William Benjamin Philpot, Hamlet Philpot

A Scrip of Salvage

From the Poems of William Philpot

William Benjamin Philpot, Hamlet Philpot

A Scrip of Salvage
From the Poems of William Philpot

ISBN/EAN: 9783744712262

Printed in Europe, USA, Canada, Australia, Japan

Cover: Foto ©Thomas Meinert / pixelio.de

More available books at **www.hansebooks.com**

A Scrip of Salvage

FROM THE POEMS

OF

WILLIAM PHILPOT, M.A., OXON.,

Sometime Vicar of South Bersted, Sussex,
Author of 'A Pocket of Pebbles,' &c.

EDITED BY HIS SON,

HAMLET PHILPOT.

✠

LONDON.

MACMILLAN AND CO.

1891.

LONDON
Printed by STRANGEWAYS AND SONS,
Tower St., Cambridge Circus, W.C.

MEMOIR.

WILLIAM PHILPOT was born at Southwold, on the coast of Suffolk, in 1823, and was the eldest son of Benjamin Philpot, Fellow of Christ's College, Cambridge, by his marriage with Charlotte, daughter of the Rev. John Vachell, rector of Littleport, Cambridgeshire. In 1828 the Rev. Benjamin Philpot, who from 1815 had been Perpetual Curate of Walpole and Southwold, was appointed Vicar-General and Archdeacon of the Isle of Man.

The boy received his earlier education at King William's College, near Castletown, but, when the Archdeacon accepted the living of Great Cressingham, Norfolk, in 1839, was sent to Dr. Cotton's house at Rugby, and was a member of the sixth form at the time of Arnold's death. Here he made the friendship of many who shared with him the enthusi-astic veneration which he retained through life for his great teacher, and who, like himself, learned to love and honour his single-minded successor, Dr. Tait.

From Rugby he went to Trinity College, Cam-bridge ; but, two years later, on being elected to an open scholarship at Worcester College, Oxford, mi-grated to a University more suited, perhaps, to his special cast of mind. The lifelong friendships here formed included those of Dean Stanley, Professor Goldwin Smith, and the future husband of his sister, the present Dean of Westminster.

In 1851 the Rev. William Philpot married the second daughter of Lieut.-Col. Obins, of co. Armagh, Ireland, who had fought under Wellington in the Peninsular War, and was among the officers who guarded Napoleon at St. Helena. In 1858 death removed the beloved wife, whose presence and memory inspired many of the poems in this volume, and to whom the First Part is dedicated by her two children.

From his marriage to the year 1865, Mr. Philpot held the incumbency of Walesby, a village on the Wolds of Lincolnshire, where he found a kindred spirit in the Vicar of the neighbouring village of

Grasby, Charles Tennyson Turner. He then retired
to Littlehampton, in Sussex, working as a private
tutor, until appointed, in 1875, by his former Master,
the late Archbishop of Canterbury, to the living of
Bersted, Bognor, which he held until his death in
1889. His tomb is under the fig-tree in a sunny
corner of the Bersted 'garden of the dead,' close by
the vicarage, church, and schools, all of which were
restored under his care. Six weeks after his son's
death, the Venerable Archdeacon also died in his
ninty-ninth year. In life and death they were not
divided.

The First Part of this volume carries out, in a
measure, a desire of its author to publish a series of
short poems suggested by the ideas which cluster
round the title 'Home'—the meeting of two hearts,
their united life, and the memories that survive
when the home has been rent by death.

Part the Second has been arranged so as to set
out in broader lines other phases of human life, its
trials and its safeguards.

The 'Sundry Reliques' have no leading motive, the
Editor wishing merely to mix advisedly the free lyric
and the more self-contained sonnet.

While such an arrangement of the poems will give
no clue to their dates, and the personal references

need in no case be pressed, the author's friends will yet find local colour, and touches, quaint or serious, to recall a life, burdened indeed with trial to its bitter end, but buoyed up by wide sympathies, and an abundance of humour and faith.

CONTENTS.

AN APOLOGY TO THE BIRDS.

PART I.

Home: Its Making and its Memories.

Contents.

PART II.

LIFE AND DEATH.

Contents.

xi

PART III.

SUNDRY RELIQUES.

Contents.

PART IV.

HYMNS.

Part the First.

—

HOME:

Its Making and its Memories.

—

To

HARRIETT GEORGINA OBINS-PHILPOT.

Died February 9, 1858.

—

Οὐ μὲν γὰρ τοῦ γε κρεῖσσον καὶ ἄρειον
ἢ ὅθ᾽ ὁμοφρονέοντε νοήμασιν οἶκον ἔχητον
ἀνὴρ ἠδὲ γυνή.   *Odyss.*, vi. 187.

A Scrip of Salvage.

TO THE BIRDS.

YE happier souls, I hark your reboant song,
    I mark your sweep and swoop so strong o' the
        wing ;
Whene'er the Spirit whirls your car along,
    Ye wheel round all creation while ye sing.
Then for your choice of phrase, if right, if wrong,
    To this—what need that any heed ye bring ?
Image and utterance round your theme will throng,
    And dance, to measure due self-marshalling.
While I, too care-beclawed, of claims the prey,
    Can all too seldom lend my soul her swing ;
Nor can I walk in poesy's sweet way,
    Except by luck and wily time-serving ;
And then, when I can somewhere steal apart,
I fail to find what words best tally with my heart.

THE TRICOLOR.

Lassie sweet, I never knew,
Till I saw it float on you,
Such a charm in red white blue,
As you stand against the sky
On your rocky balcony ;
And the breezes past you blowing
Set your rosy face aglowing,
Set your sunlit locks aflowing
Down your white neck's snowy showing
Fair beyond all saying—sweet beyond all knowing ;
What a beauteous banner flies
From your cheek and neck and eyes ;
Never till to-day I knew
What the tricolor could do.

VENUS VICTRIX.

So there, my perilous warriouresse, you pose
At once Love's champion and his dearest prize ;
Oh ! in what proud array your beauty goes !
See what rare levin flashes from your eyes !
Your words far worse than all artilleries,
As though you ranked me with your deadliest foes ;
Your beauty vaunting what your grace denies,
Why draw me, dare me, to a fatal close ?
Or else why wear that ventayle on your brow,
Your wimpled locks a plumèd burganet,
A tower impregnable your neck of snow,
On either cheek a blood-red banneret,
Your breasts—brave outworks which yoú dare me
          scale—
Well ! Love be dayesman—if I fail, I fail.

TOO FAR ABOVE ME.

FOR me, in sooth, I ween
Far simpler had it been
To roam the woodland through
From prime till latest dew,
Lifting lamentful palms
To win to my poor arms
The fairest fair of all the Dryads ;
I might as lief
Have clomb the tip of Teneriffe
And crooked my knees
To try and please
The sweetest influence of all the Pleiads ;
Them might I haply have drawn down to love me,
But thou for ever art too far above me.

LOVE'S 'PROPOSITIONS.'

i.

THE UNIVERSAL AND THE PARTICULAR.

'TWAS not a general love of that fair kind
Whose rank encircles a particular thee—
That universal rather storms my mind
Led on by thy particularity.
Shall any one tell me now that love is blind,
Seeing that all that fair infinity
Of nymphal possibles was massed behind
Unseen till when thy love revealed it me?
I caught through thee some glimmering glamourie
That now and then further or nearer shined,
But what men meant by all that amourie
I knew not, nor to question was inclined ;
The general gender only took mine eye
When marshalled by thy special captaincy.

*   *   *

ii.

MY 'UNIVERSAL NEGATIVE.'

YOU may not speak to me, for, when you do,
You swoon me with the music-motioned air ;
You may not smile on me, for that rare view
Upsweeps me but to swamp me in despair ;
I must not watch you weeping, for that too
Wasteth what cheer may linger anywhere ;
Pray close your eyes, for when you look me through
There comes a rush of life I cannot bear ;
You slay me when you laugh or when you weep,
Whether you choose to rest or else to move ;
You slay me if you wake, or if you sleep,
For, while 'tis yours to live, 'tis mine to love—
And yet, if thus all round you cease, you die !
And so, my life would follow presently.

*　　*　　*

iii.

A 'PARTICULAR NEGATIVE.'

NOW to what angle of the habited star
I know not whether least 'twere scathe to fly;
Flee where I would, what nook is found so far
But thy dear form would beam for ever nigh?
Should I not bear thee clear before mine eye,
Couch where I might? what seas could rear a bar,
Yea, though the witchery of thy gaze to mar,
They piled them clambering Himalayas high?
But—only let the trump of catholic doom
Rive into chasmy gulphs this ordered crust,
Plunge all that can be shivered into gloom,
Haloed with fiery wreathes of discreate dust.
Why, then, I know, 'twere safe and well for me
To catch thy palm and face the judge with thee.

A REMONSTRANCE WITH WALLER.

Go, blowing rose,
Tell them that note thee, young or old,
'Tis better they be close than bold.
   Say in thy half-blown days
   Men gave thee fuller praise
When with meek care thou didst thy heart enfold ;
Tell me, O full-blown rose, while now
   With most unbashful brow
Thou openest out upon the common air,
   Thy beauty disarrayed,
   Thy mystery all displayed,
We cannot deem thee half so fair—
There was the sign thou hadst begun to fade ;
O blowing rose, it had been truer art
To keep some lovely leaves close folded round thy
      heart.

AFTER ANACREON.

'Α βάρβιτος δὲ χορδαῖς
Ἔρωτα μοῦνον ἠχεῖ.

FAIN I was to sing of fate
Power and wealth and war and state ;
Ramparts built and cities burned,
Empires reared and kings o'erturned—
   But my lyre refused to move
   Any music but of Love.

Yestermorn I changed the strings ;
Then I changed the shell itself ;
But my new one only sings
Like that old one on the shelf ;
   Be it so—'twere vain to move
   Any music but of Love.

"Αγε, ζωγράφων ἄριστε κ.τ.λ.

'He falls to such perusal of my face
As he would draw it.'—*Shakspeare.*

PRINCE of painters, come, I pray,
Paint my love, for, though away,
King of craftsmen, you can well
Paint what I to thee can tell.
First, her hair you must indite
Dark, but soft as summer night ;
Hast thou no contrivance whence
To make it breathe its frankincense ?
Rising from her rounded cheek
Let thy pencil duly speak,
How below that purpling night
Glows her forehead ivory-white.
Mind you neither part nor join
Those sweet eyebrows' easy line ;
They must merge, you know, to be
In separated unity.
Painter, draw, as lover bids,
Now the dark line of the lids ;
Painter, now 'tis my desire,
Make her glance from very fire,
Make it as Athene's blue,
Like Cythera's liquid too ;

Now to give her cheeks and nose,
Milk must mingle with the rose ;
Her lips be like persuasion's made,
To call for kisses they persuade ;
And for her delicious chin,
O'er and under and within,
And round her soft neck's Parian wall,
Bid fly the graces, one and all.
For the rest, enrobe my pet
In her faint clear violet ;
But a little truth must show
There is more that lies below.
Hold ! thou hast her—that is she.
Hush ! she's going to speak to me.

NEVER, OR FOR EVER.

SEEING I love thee, lady, for ever,
I know thou must always be with me—or never.
  Never—lady—never,
    Or else for ever and ever.

THE ARROW ON THE VANE.

THOU art that vane, and, lady, I the wind,
That all thy changes well have learned to find;
Constant I keep thy winged inconstant dart,
With golden barb straight pointed to my heart;
Why wilt thou never let it leave the string,
New life in death to this poor heart to bring?

MY PROMOTION TO HER MINISTRY.

' Tuus, O regina, quid optes
Explorare labor, mihi jussa capessere fas est.'—*Virgil.*

As some poor wight, who inly hopes his Queen
    May lift him to some office i' the State,
Trusting each morn her mandate may be seen
    Sealed with her battling beasts and royal date ;
Yet, conscious what imperial labours mean,
    And trembling to misjudge self-estimate,
Dares make no move, nor use a come-between,
    Nor takes one step such post to supplicate ;
So I beneath thy pleasure wait and wait,
    Hoping the happy hour thy smile serene
May call me to approach thy palace-gate,
    O Sovereign Lady, my most gracious Queen !
I languish, longing for that little sign,
To touch thy sceptre and avow me thine.

'*THIS BUD OF LOVE.*'

ROM. AND JUL.

UPON the way I saw her go,
  I find thee ;—didst thou fall by chance ?
I gave her thee, full well I know,
  Say, rosebud, 'backward' or 'advance'?

Hid in thy leaves I fain would find
  What, when she eyed thee last, she meant ;
It was, I know not why, unkind
  To lose thee, even *sans* intent.

If thou by very chance wert lost,
  The while my sweet-heart never knew,
'Twere thus with one who prized thee most,
  I blame not her, I blame not you.

But what an if in pettish scoff,
  Not knowing I should pass this way,
Both thee and me she thus cast off ?
  Why, then, I hate this bitter day.

Nay, I bethink me, rosebud, now,
  'I mean to come this way,' I said ;
She tossed me here no doubt to show
  She scorned me !—would that I were dead.

But, lo ! who comes ? lie there, poor flower,
   I'll cast me 'neath this hedgerow grass,
And I shall know within the hour,
   Come death, come life, what comes to pass.

She stoops — she peers with tearful eye,
   Retracing inch by inch her way ;
She'll surely see thee by-and-by !
   Not yet will I regret to-day.

She sees thee — mark, her thankful face
   Upbrightens in the happy sun !
Who ever wore such winning grace ?
   What sweeter thing was ever done ?

She clasps dear hands ; she leaps to take
   My token from the common way ;
She plants it — all for my poor sake,
   By the sweet heart I win to-day.

'Twas well, my little rose, I own,
   To fall by good Sir Isaac's law,
For else I had not seen and known
   The pleasant things I know and saw.

To-morrow, with thy kindness charmed,
   We'll kiss thy core for this kind part,
And withered thou shalt lie embalmed
   Within the archives of my heart.

THE CLOSED TRIPTYCH.

THY face is like some triptych fair
Double enclosed by the kind Master's care ;
On either folding door the same great hand
Hath set such limning as to make one yearn
With much impatient earnestness to earn
The great delight to see
What inner grace is worth an outer case like thee.

THE FUTURE OF LOVE.

THY face, thy grace, thy form, are such
    As saw I ne'er before,
But if I love thy beauty much
    I love thy bounty more.

Thy spirit speaks in every line,
    Thy dust is lit with fire,
To fence it as with sword divine
    From creeping vague desire.

Thy beauty is of such a cast,
    My love must needs be true,
Who loves in thee what may not last
    Must love the lasting too.

The lovesomeness of all thou art
    The dearer grows to me,
In that it draws my watchful heart
    To love what thou wilt be.

From love to love thy pathway shines ;
    And, as thy days go on,
Unless what mortal is declines,
    There will be nothing gone.

On earth how sweet it were to live
  With that in thee which dies,
So with thee dying to arrive
  At thine eternities.

Yet so th' Eternal bears thee on
  Through every change of time,
The dust downshook by thy death-song
  Must leave thee in thy prime.

Such power of Heaven reigns through thee now,
  The years may work their will,
Who live to mourn will joy to know
  With thee 'tis Heaven still.

A Heaven enhanced by full delight
  Of commune with the blest ;
May I be there to share the sight,
  Thou dearest of the best.

THE HOUR AND THE WOMAN.

HAD I but wrought my posy yesterday,
I might have chased it in a fairer ring ;
Or else, should I forbear and say my say
To-morrow, I might chant some worthier thing !
Who knows the causes that come clustering—
The sun, the veiny wine, in hidden play
Around some fancy caught upon the wing
To shape its flight in least unhappy way?
Grant heaven to me, when to my love I sing,
And think to court her in beseeching lay,
All modes and measures may combine to bring
Their winning aid ; then bid, dear muse, I pray,
Shine sun, dance blood, blow breeze, and words up-
        spring,
So leaning, listening, she may breathe me 'yea.'

'*SHE IS LIKE UNTO THE MERCHANT SHIPS.*'

PROV. xxxi. 14.

THOU wast a pinnace in the fairest sort,
All on the sea with gale and sunshine playing ;
I saw, and, seeing, longed to be thy port,
And sought to make my roadstead worth thy staying ;
From this lone coast, in sorrow long delaying,
I watched the fancy-freedom of thy sport ;
Vain was my loud lament and all my praying,
Vain the sad signals flying from my fort ;
But thou—thou knewest all my heart was thine ;
And that was well—tho' once it 'gan to fail—
When, lo ! by reason of some breeze divine,
Full on my soul thy beauty bore full sail ;
And down my streets and quays, sweet pinnace mine,
My best affections thronged to interchange ' All hail ! '

THE INFLOW OF LOVE.

How great an hour, how gently past,
   It came as things eternal do
That turn between my unlove's last
   And the first thought I had of you.

So masterful, so full of change,
   So fraught with unexperienced power
To tell through my eternal range ;
   And yet how silent was the hour.

You moved me like a strain of song
   That sways through yielding waves of air;
Or as a ship that steals along
   And shifts a here into a there.

Or as the tide one summer eve
   Turns silent ebb to silent flow,
I know not how and scarce believe—
   You stole upon me even so.

Or as the inflow of a book,
   That sweeps away a foolish creed,
So with the magic of your look
   You showed me you had met my need.

You with the sweetness of your love,
   And all the charm of your controul,
Came as a thought that from above
   Converts the purpose of a soul.

As on a man that faints and dies
   The peace of Paradise will ope,
So like my better life you rise
   Beyond my best imagined hope.

SPRING WEATHER.

I KNOW a life much like an April day,
Here hung with clouds and there alive with sun ;
And neither in the selfsame mood will stay,
While 'neath her heaven the winds of feeling run ;
So all is dark where one short hour agone
Were thousand sunbeams lovingly at play ;
And presently, I trow, smiles many a one
Will chase the grief that now can lower so grey.
Such weather to my mind is fairer far
Than where the simmering hours all summer are ;
Thy sorrow, girl, is more than duly sad,
But then thy gladness is divinely glad ;
And soon, methinks, a change will light thy brow,
And all thine hours be what the best are now.

Heidelberg.

LOVE APPLES.

AND dost thou wonder, love, if soon
  I shall be as I am to-day?
If passion is a passing boon
  Which winds that bring can bear away?

Thy fears, my tender little one,
  If true in part, are false in whole ; ·
For, grant that passion will be gone,
  Hath nothing quickened in the soul?

Put case, in Nature's ripening growth
  Some flowers of feeling we forget ;
I plight thee, sweet-apple, my troth,
  The fruit is now already set.

Love's orchard, trust me, is akin
  To that the Western maids of old
So duly husbanded—within
  The apples are of purest gold.

No bound of blooth my plat shall bear ;
  And every tree, one fruitage done,
Shall show, each month of all the year,
  Another and another one.

And as we gather from the wise
  That feelings fall as fashions grow,
While those sweet usages arise
  Fresh feelings shall about them blow.

AIR SCULPTURE.

i.

OH, would that, for the while I see thee there
So sweetly poised before my pondering eyne,
I could but suade the swift recurrent air
To leave the limits of that pose of thine
Clear uninvaded all along thy line !
'Tis something strange that round a space so fair
The element should not hang with feeling fine,
Yet not so strange as not to so repair.
Oh, sweet warm space, oh, idol of delight,
Would I not rear thee, whither I might go,
Of all materials most rich and bright
A grot for temple and for studio !
But, since this air is common and unkind,
That pose and poise for fane must use my mind.

ii.

To think the hasty air must fill that space
Where thou dost beam in all thy beauty now,
Nor pay the least regard to that dear place
Warmed by that heaving bosom, that white brow;
Yea, in upon thine ever vading face,
And on the sweetest features that I know,
Without a touch of due retiring grace
Will, like a tide on summer shore, reflow;
And though some other shape of ambient air
Displace thou wilt—yet that, alas ! will be
To my sore sorrow far, far otherwhere,
And never once be hung around by me ;
Yea, to my smart, there yet must come a day
When no fond air will clasp thee any way.

iii.

I deem that I shall die when thou art gone ;
For, even when I muse on thy retreat,
And body forth the being left alone,
I feel my heart already fail to beat :
The sense of losing all my life had won,
Of being swept from off these earthy feet,
And losing memory of life and heat,
Fills me with dread of being clean undone !
How I shall now this dreary coming on
Of dissolution stay, I barely weet.
Come let me plant thee by the viewless throne
Of Him Whom, tho' I see not, yet 'tis meet
And right to trust upon that great white seat—
Seen never, ever loved, till life be new begun.

HER RETURN.

WEARY for springtime waiteth the year ;
So thy beloved one waits for thee here ;
As craves the bare ash for its sap to arise,
Crave I to quaff the dear light of thine eyes ;
As for the land breeze panteth the sea,
So I am yearning, my darling, for thee ;
As for the sea-breeze longeth the shore,
So I am sighing to see thee once more ;
As the dry harbour mouth waits for the tide,
Wait I to find thee once more by my side ;
Like friends that are crowding the edge of a quay
Throng my affections with welcome for thee.

As the ship beareth full sail to the shore,
So thou art coming to leave me no more ;
As the full ocean floods up to the creek,
So doth she enter, the soul that I seek ;
As the sea-breezes blow fresh on the sand,
She freshens the brow of my heart as I stand ;
As the land-breezes rush over the sea,
Laden with fragrance, returns she to me ;
As the sweet sap to the end of the bough,
So through and through me, returning one, thou ;
Like the full flood of the spring to the earth,
Thou with thy sweetness and beauty and worth ;
The doors of our house, let me fling them apart,
Come back to our home and come back to my heart.

Walesby.

SUMMER DAYS.

WHEN the crocus' fiery tongue
   Bids the wreaths of snow begone ;
When the cherry, quick with song,
   Throws her tinted bravery on ;
March or May, 'tis one to me,
   None, my love, is fresh like thee.

When the sun is all the hearth
   Half the world will care to know ;
When the golden-bosomed earth
   Shimmers, all her glebes aglow ;
June or August, all is one,
   None, my love, is like thee—none.

When the last o' the gleaner crew
   Spoils the wreck no more for shame,
When the leaves of sunburnt hue
   Shivering steal to whence they came ;
Month by month, it seems to me,
   None hath tenderness like thee.

When the Living maid as dead
   Sleeps beneath her snowy pall ;
When the merry hearth is red
   And the home is all to all ;
None, my love, is like thee, none,
   Summer days are every one.

ON THE FALL OF AN HOUR-GLASS.

*[To his love, whose forehead had been scarred by the fall of
the same.]*

As one who feels the rossignol
Regale the listening groves with song,
And well the fulness of his soul
In measured torrent all night long,

So I with thee, love, by my side;
Such harmony of heart redounds,
I dance upon my life's high tide,
And all my day runs diamonds.

Time had not dropped that sorry glass,
Nor found the heart to wound thy brow,
Hadst thou but taught him then to pass
The hours that thou hast taught him now.

Or knew he what should come to us?
So, fretful at his hopeless task,
Poor petulance, defaced thee thus,
Full loth to grant what love should ask?

He felt thy life could laugh to scorn
The lobes in that his palsied hand ;
That there was something to be born
Would need no more his grains of sand.

Ah, yes ! the green-eyed dotard knew,
When first he saw thee in thy prime,
A love should run between us two,
Which should not thank the count of time.

Nor yet would all the shores of earth
Mete any measure for the love,
That, breaking forth in better birth,
Would prove itself immense above.

So Time may chafe, and Time may rail,
And Time's last glass in shivers lie,
While thou and I crowd snowy sail
Across the free Eternity.

Brussels.

EMIGRANTS.

i.

Πατρὶς γάρ ἐστι πᾶσ' ἵν' ἂν πράττῃ τις εὖ.

THE old world starves behind them, their old home
Clung to and loved while they might love and cling;
How were those hearts enfranchised thus to roam
Where'er the winds of heaven their fortunes fling?
Hard was it to disown each well-known thing,
And face the perilous breadth of friendless foam;
What keen distresses o'er these natures come,
To force them leave their hearth and friends and king!
What matter? life beneath another sun
Is more than death beneath their childhood's one;
Never have he and she so loved before
As now, when other loves are seen no more;
Never are hearts so riveted together
As theirs that battle through the boisterous weather.

ii.

'Nulli certa domus.'

SEQUESTERED from the crew, as best they may,
In sunny nook beside the breezy prow,
By use of voyage made familiar now,
How sweet through all the long Atlantic day,
'Neath the broad heaven's shadow-shifting brow,
To list the changeful waters in their play,
Which falling off in furrows leave a way,
While the winds chant as only they know how ;
Thrice blest to gaze into each other's eyes,
In idle interval of destinies,
And read as in the volume of the book
Trust and dependence there in every look ;
To make each other's breast by turns a pillow,
And dream of golden homes beyond the billow.

iii.

'Cœlum, non animum, mutant qui trans mare currunt.'
Horace.

So love the twain, as only those can know,
Who winged as seeds upon the westward wind,
The blue above them and the green below,
Fare forth with resolute heart and even mind,
Before them ocean, home and friends behind.
They know not rightly to what land they go,
But this at least they know — that Heaven is kind,
And Faith and Hope and Love endear them so,
As none can tell but two such souls as they,
And more than e'en their own sweet sense can say.
The uncertain sea their only known abode ;
They lean each on the other, both on God ;
And all the fret and change of this world's weather
But twine their twi-une fates more fast together.

SPRING FLOWERS.

' Qualem virgineo demessum pollice florem
Seu mollis violæ seu languentis hyacinthi. '

VIRG.

OF all the flowers rising now,
    Thou only saw'st the head
Of that unopened drop of snow
    I placed beside thy bed.

In all the blooms that blow so fast,
    Thou hast no further part,
Save those, the hour I saw thee last,
    I laid above thy heart.

Two snowdrops for our boy and girl,
    A primrose blown for me,
Wreathed with one often-played-with curl
    From each bright head for thee.

And so I graced thee for thy grave,
    And made these tokens fast
With that old silver heart I gave,
    My first gift—and my last.

'MY BELOVED IS MINE AND I AM HIS.'

NOTHING can harm thee,
Nothing alarm thee,
Nothing can vex thee,
Nothing perplex thee,
Nothing oppress thee,
Nothing distress thee :
For Jesus doth bless thee,
The Spirit caress thee,
The Father possess thee.

Βῆ δ'ἀκεὼν παρὰ θῖνι.

PRETTY shells we find no more,
For thine eyes have left the shore,
Now is no one there whose feet
Seem to ocean maidens meet
That around them they should fling
The choice they kept for thee of every pleasing thing.

Hoarser, sadder grew the wail
Of the melancholy sea,
When he found the music fail
That he used to learn from thee ;
Treble of thy thrilling strain
Toned the thunder of his main,
Ah, me, could he, could I, but hear it once again !

What flowers can we light on now—
Weeds they call them—of the sea ?
They have gone, I know not how,
Or they come not missing thee ;
Time, love, was, when on the beach
Strolling slowly towards the sun
We would find in ready reach
Light-steeped agates many a one;
But, oh, without thee now alone I light on none.

Every crystal, gem, and shell
Shrink to some concealing cell,
Blown there by the sighful wind
Of my sadly-moaning mind,
That caring not to look forgets the way to find.
'Twas the line of thy dear eye
On the sparkling shingle bent
Wont to fall in days gone by
On the jewels spray-besprent
And the rays that shot and gleamed
From those wells beneath thy brow
Such a store of radiance beamed
That those poor stones we picked are shining in it now.
Into such a dye you cast them,
Transfusing them, not flowing past them—
Such lights you gave to stay there and to last them.
The power of seeing all things sweet
Is somewhere sure behind the eye,
And, though they lie about my feet,
I gaze and gaze, yet not descry—
Love in a lonely heart knows best the reason why.

Νῦν δ'ἐστι μάκαιρα δαίμων.

Eur.

HOW art thou now, sweet spirit? when I ask,
O'er all my face and soul dim darkness grows;
I feel my eyes grow moist before the task
Forth peering to yon land that no man knows.
Yet Some One tells my spirit thou dost bask
In some warm light that comes and never goes,
Bathing thy being—though a cloud must mask
For me the glory that about thee flows;
Where'er the Perfect is, I feel art thou,
And I shall know it, though I know not now;
Plant of the Father's planting, born to blow
Among the fairest blooms the best can show—
Then, as I muse, I find some shadows flee
Feeling the touch of light down-drawn from thee.

AT FRESHWATER.

ALONE, alone I make my moan
Lonely—though not, I know, alone—
For thou, my love, art gone—art gone.

I hear the night tide swelling, failing,
The deeps in chorus each the other hailing—
Strophe, anti-strophe of wailing;

Beach unto beach in breaking murmurs sighing,
Voices of night along the headlands dying,
Far unto near in fainter falls replying.

Through the lone night, my love, my heart is waking,
Thousands of thoughts along my soul are breaking,
Where art thou love—to me no answer making?

The moon was like a burning ball
Flattened against the round blue wall,
Seaward as though in act to fall.

No golden chain as yet she flung
Netted as now the waves among,
Alone in heaven a while she hung;

But now, how beautiful to see
That road of gold from her to me—
Oh, could I look on her with thee!

Thus, Heavenly Father, let there lie
For me some pathway to the sky,
To be uptravelled by-and-by.

Thou hast my chosen spirit there
Fairer than ever she was fair ;
Thou hast her, though I know not where.

The moon keeps climbing up the sky,
And brighter ever seems to lie
That broad way of tranquillity.

As she ascends yon heavenly hill,
Her influence seems to hold at will
The sea, like these sweet slumberers, still.

Lo ! as the black onflowing tide
Beneath her influence comes to glide,
That dark soul seems all glorified.

Her orb above my roof hath clomb,
I see not whither she hath come,
That pathway tells me of her home.

Grant me, O God, the ear to hark,
The eye to see, the heart to mark
Thy parables to light from dark.

i.

SWEET castle at whose gate so long I lay
Leaguering thy moat with all artillery
Of patient love, and setting in array
The prance and tramp of all contingency
Of thought and fancy; sending day by day
Much overture of courteous heraldry;
Hoping for years to win the happy way
To the deep doors of thy full treasury
Morning by morning on thy battled towers
What blazonry of beauty blinded me !
While terrible thy banners minded me
That only for the brave were those bright bowers—
Then most triumphant wast thou when most tender,
Strong in defiance, stronger in surrender.

ii.

'Indocilis pauperiem pati.'

AND so a prisoner at thy feet I fell
When thou didst touch me with imperial hand,
And with most gracious bosom think it well
To invest me there and then with full command
Of thine and thee—thy castles and thy land,
With treasures past what any queen could tell :
Thy flag by the fond breeze so boldly fanned
I did not find it in my heart to quell,
But mine I straightway hoisted by its side
O'er thy sweet champaign in one air to ride ;
I could not take one single archive-key,
But followed, as I could, led on by thee ;
And thus I found thee rich beyond belief—
Now am I poor indeed or only rich in grief.

I DREAMED, her babe upon her breast,
Here she might lie and calmly rest
Her happy eyes on that far hill
That backs the landscape fresh and still.

I hoped her thoughts would thrid the boughs
Where careless birds on love carouse,
And gaze those apple-blossoms through
To revel in the boundless blue.

But now her faculty of sight
Is elder sister to the light,
And travels free and unconfined
Through dense and rare, through form and mind.

Or else her life to be complete
Hath found new channels full and meet—
Then, oh, what eyes are leaning o'er -
If fairer than they were before.

i.

SHE sailed around the harbour of my heart,
Embraced and glassed within my tranquil bay,
Laden with love, whereof no little part
Here on my wharves I can with sighs display,
The rest not yet unfreighted for my mart
Is lost, or hidden till some happier day;
For two short months ago to my sore smart
A stress of sudden weather on her lay,
And she, my only barque, with all she bore
Sunk in a night into unsounded sleep,
How deeply laden with the bounteous store
Of all she brought ;—so here I wait and weep ;
Ah ! what shall bring me to my beggared shore
The treasures buried in that treacherous deep ?

ii.

'Απ' οὖν τέκνων σῶν πημονὴν εἴργοι ϑεός.

EUR.

WHAT have I rescued from this wreck of mine ?
Here are two little lives whom thou hadst landed
Fetched from afar, at desperate risk of thine,
For then thy lovely shape was all but stranded—
And they and I beside this sea divine
Now roam and gather what the waves, commanded
By Him who rules them, have in mercy handed
From the dark depth of yonder deadly brine.
And mostly these are images that rise
From the dear past where they were calmly lying,
Thoughts, looks, words, works and attitudes sup-
     plying,
A funeral feast for silent memories,
From the first hour I saw thy living eyes
To that last morning when I felt them dying.

I LOVE this air because it sank and rose
With those last tides of that beloved breast ;
I love the sun that lit thee to repose
Leaving his chamber in the desolate East ;
The under world felt darkness round it close,
As I when once thy life for me had ceased,
Though having soon forgot thy night of woes
Thy light with his from one rich morn increased ;
Night too I love, whose solemn watches passed
To sound of words, thy sweetest for thy last ;
I love those birds that helped to sing thee up
When thou hadst met thine hour and drank thy cup ;
Thou having been below art now above,—
Thus earth and heaven are full of all I love.

SHINE AND SHADOW.

NEVER o'er the lawns again,
To my bitter pain,
Light, awakened by her tread,
Copies her from foot to head
Passing through the open glade,
First in shape and then in shade;—
So that her never-coming now has greyed
All the sunny lawn in shade
Darker by far than that her fairy form had made,
     Now she is gone.

> ' Nec solos tangit Atreidas
Iste dolor.'
>
> VIRG.

FAR from his fellows there he sat apart
By the hoarse margent of the restless sea,
And o'er its wine-dark waters flung his heart
And reached his hands in lovelorn fantasy ;
So I athwart the vast Eternity,
Whereby I saw my own Briseis start,
In moods between despair and ecstasy
Throw useless gaze and cypher many a chart
Of her imagined way with trembling hand
On the lone flats of this unfruitful sand—
Sands of my soul still shimmering with the glow
Of all the bliss that o'er them used to flow—
My tide hath ebbed, my day-star now hath set,
My love hath passed, and here I linger yet.

AMORIS CUNÆ.

I THINK there never could have passed a day
In all thy life when I had loved thee not ;
Had I come hovering in boyish way
Above the curtains of thine earliest cot,
Why, even then, thou half o' my life, God wot
I should have drawn to thee in some dear play.
Thy sweet eyes could not have been quite forgot
Beaming 'forget-me-nots' thou couldst not say.
How strange that, waxing in the selfsame earth,
I saw thee not till summers twenty-five
Had brought thee nurture from the hour of birth
And saved thee, for my love at last, alive.
Lo ! now again th' Eternal Home doth own thee,
May long long Heaven repay not having earlier
        known thee.

SHALL I DISTURB YOU?

Ah ! airy light rat-a-tat of rounded point
Of right forefinger's pink recurvèd joint,
Held for a moment, my dearie,
As if in affectionate query
Whether in quest of my honey-store
Busily buried in flowers of lore
Thy gracious advent might not aid me more—
'Tis but a memory—twenty and seven
Summers since then have had thee in heaven,
Yet am I fain to hie and discover
If on the panel of the chamber door
No little dent of the fairy finger,
No little tread in the corridor,
Of her who came to her wedded lover
Still may in any way chance to linger.
   Dupe that I am ! what fancy could venture
Ever to deem that so fine an indenture
Could bide the usage of so rough a stage,
Fourth of a cómplete century of mine age ?
As if the rattle and rude battery
Of all the years with their mad devilry
Had not for ever clean effaced,
If aught could ever have been traced,

That impact delicate and sweet
And the soft tread of unobtrusive feet—
And yet I ween that rat-a-tat
And tenderly approaching pit-a-pat
Were not so slight, so readily outworn,
But that to-night and eke every morn
It can as clearly speak upon the door
Of this poor heart and on my temple floor
As when was made the primal sound
Whose echoes till to-day redound :
  The form I could clasp has been banished
And the ear-caught signs they are vanished,
But she and all that belongs to her
—Witness all of my songs for her—
One with my life for evermore
Bide in my soul resounding as before.

Bersted.

BEHIND THE VEIL.

How slight a veil could hide a view how vast !
The tenderest distances of days gone by,
The purest states of all my holiest past,
The clearest works of downgone energy,
The palace of sweet love, which one wild blast
Shattered and scattered from mine earthly eye,
Leaving me nothing while my life shall last
But this veiled vista of old memory.
How thin a screen, it seems, before it hung !
For, plucking as I passed this delicate bloom,
A whiff of the fine perfume that it flung
Blew back a quarter-century of gloom :
The effluence of this yellow rose reswung
A curtain thick, methought, as folds of doom.

Part the Second.

—

LIFE AND DEATH.

LIFE.

Χρὴ, ἐφ' ὅσον ἐνδέχεται, ἀθανατίζειν.

Ar.

WHAT is thy life? true 'tis a part enjoyment
Through thy few faculties that find employment
Along this rocky, sandy, toilsome march;—
But what is life? look upward to the arch
Whose boundless ether, bending down above thee,
Symbols the Power who made thee but to love thee;
What is thy life? a boundless expectation:
Nothing, bless God, can cancel thy creation;
If thou wast nought, if nought could be, before,
Being once here, thou canst be nought no more,
Once with thy foot upon the shore of Time,
    No billows of the desolate sea
Can cheat thee of thy power to grow sublime
    And cause thee not to be;
Lift up thy heart and voice to bless
Him that hath snatched thee out from nothingness,
And by a breath thy name and place hath given,
Heir of a kingdom, and that kingdom heaven;
Be wise;—and look not closer than is meet
Upon the evils strewn around thy feet;

They are but passing ; death is overcome,
And none of these, when once thou art at home,
Will be at all remembered ; fix thy gaze
Upon the coming issue of thy days ;—
How shall a man not leap for joy to be,
Whose life is bearing him along to see
Days of the Son of man, and nature's birth,
That coming heaven and this bridal earth ?

ÆGYPTIAN BONDS.

My Nile, I lie all Delta to thy flow—
O'er me and up me sweep with all thy wave :
Have I not seeds of lingering life below
That through the long, long drouth thy refluence
    crave ?
My bread is buried here in loamy grave,
And ere thy coming what have I to show ?
With sweet redundance thou my being lave,
That what my harvest is I soon may know.
Have I not cast beneath thee all I have,
To find it after many days, or no ;
And yet—ah ! me—tho' now my hopes be brave
I fear I may that desperate all forego—
For what if after all no seeds I save—
But reeds of empty verse to voice my woe ?

LEAD US NOT INTO TEMPTATION.

PRAY Heaven to me there never supervene,
Before I pass to some impassive mode,
The dread conjuncture of some pleasure seen
With absence of my Lord from this abode ;
Nay rather, sweet proceeder from our God,
So ever keep thy gracious stand between
The rush of visibles and this frail clod,
That I be ne'er o'erpowered to deed of sin !
Hold off the perilous press of circumstance
From access to these precincts of my soul,
And blacken to my view the giddy dance
Of gauzy fancies ; kill their fell control ;
Pray let me pass and so be safely Thine
Ere some wild boar break in upon Thy vine.

THE SIREN ISLE.

i.

'Te sæpe vocanti
Duram, difficilis mane.'
HOR.

I MAY not touch one creek of all the shore
Of thee, thou dainty, love-begirdled isle,
Tho' fragrance breathe around thee from the store
Of varied spices all the precious while;
Yea, though a gracious welcome in thy smile
Allure my prow those inlets to explore,
And though a little movement and light guile
On my frail part makes thee thine own no more.
Yet in the name of Heaven I hold aloof
And merely coast about thee—though, alas!
My silly craft was never tempest-proof,
I crowd all canvas, stand to sea, and pass,
For, should I touch, I know that it would be
Ravage and wreck to thee, fair isle, and me.

ii.

Κάλλος κακῶν ὕπουλον.

Some sturdier crew would see thy ruins' reek,
And, if in pity they should turn thy way
Would catch disastrous wails and hear thee speak
Lamentful tales of anguish and dismay;
Then would they curse the man that was so weak
To test the ravishment of this old lay
That now in languishment so sweet and meek
Shivers my sail with touch of speed's delay.
Farewell; infect as heretofore the breeze,
And lure and sing and sign and sweep and smile,
Spread out for other craft thy damned wile,
But let me veer upon the path I please,
'Twere only for the hour 'twould do me ease
To dally in thy creeks, thou fair enchantress isle.

PRIMUM MOBILE.

GUIDE me, Thou Sire of lights, like yon small star ;
Bent tho' I be on my particular way,
Keeping my own set course as best I may,
Let me not clash with any lives that are ;
Let me have heed that no one near or far,
Caring to note my circlings night or day,
May come before Thee with a plaint and say
That any other moving life I mar—
And hear me yet again one grace implore ;
Impart such mastering motion to my soul—
So hear me, Heaven, I pray Thee, evermore,
That I, a part, move on with Thee, the whole ;
Oh, sweep me with Thy universe divine,
And let my little round be borne along with Thine.

YOUR orbit bears you near to mine,
    But never, never may we meet,
Mine never can be one with thine,
    The semblance is a dear deceit ;
Were I to choose and take thy range,
We clash and perish in the change.

You moving yonder shine on me
    And cheer me with your kindly light,
Perchance I shed a ray on thee —
    We orb in one another's sight,
Yet may not meet till life be done,
And both be swept into the sun.

I WILL TELL THEE THEN.

i.

IF I loved thee but in measure,
   I would draw thy lips to mine,
Tell thee I had found my treasure,
   Swear that I was ever thine ;
But I love thee far too well
Thus to thee my love to tell.

ii.

Therefore if I stand apart,
   Seem to rank thee with the rest,
Holding down a swelling heart
   Firm within a duteous breast,
Thus much, maiden, I will tell,
'Tis because I love thee well.

iii.

Thou and I must love asunder
   Till our hearts lie dust with dust ;
Then, when passing things lie under,
   Then made perfect with the just,
Where the laws of God and men
   Clash not — I will tell thee then.

THE BEST PART BUT PART AT BEST.

Ψυχρὰν μὲν οἶμαι τέρψιν.

Eur.

E'EN tho' I love thee with the best I have,
'Tis hard to love thee with a part of me ;
All else I am and all I have and know
Come pressing in for sacrifice ; what then ?
Since few of these are either mine to give
Or thine to take—behold I offer none.
I am a statue in a garden-plat,
And all thy lights from morn to tearful eve
Fly over me and round me, but my lips
Move not, and both my arms in act to reach
Stay stone-arrested, till the close of time.
So hard it is to love thee but in part,
Yea, though I love thee with this best—my heart.

PRESENCE AND ABSENCE.

'Illam absens absentem auditque videtque.'
VIRG.

WHEN you are here, I'm confident I live,
  Pleased with what passes 'neath the blue profound;
When you are gone, what reckoning can I give
  Of all the happy turns 'neath all its round?
When you are here, I hunt on every ground,
  And hidden thoughts with keen delight retrieve;
When you are gone, I slink from sight and sound,
  I doze, blink, start, and half my customs leave;
When you are here, then also here am I;
  When you are gone, I wonder where I am;
When you are here, I hope I shall not die;
  When you are gone, all issues seem the same:
And yet, though this be so, my wanted one,
'Tis well that thou art here, and better thou art gone.

SYMPLEGADES.

I KNOW two pleasant wooded capes
   That seen afar we say must meet,
For each the other overlaps,
   Each seems to kiss the other's feet.
But, ah ! too true, if nearer seen,
The envious river rolls between.

So you and I together move
   Within each other's daily view,
And few, I think, could better love
   Than you love me and I love you.
But yet asundered, love, we are ;
How near we live—but yet how far.

Μάλθακον ὀμμάτων βέλος.

THE gentle fire of that new eye
Around his heart as harmless played
As lightnings from a summer sky
On some sere trunk already laid.

THE WRITING ON THE WALL.

HE wrote gold stars on yonder round blue wall
  That rings horizons-full of loveliness ;
He breathed the laws of life and crowned them all
  In breathing one who should them all possess ;
It was His pleasure from His store to call
  Whatever most this living soul might bless ;
We, made with choice to stand, made choice to fall ;
  Yet even so doth Heaven regard us less ?
Nay, with a patient sorrow all the while,
  He lets us feel a sunshine in His smile ;
He fills our hearts with gladness, and for food
  With daily dole delights to do us good ;—
Oh, how would Earth and Man run o'er with Beauty,
If, as He holds to Love, we held to Duty.

Frankfort.

You heavens, like doves, in duteous circles roll,
  O stars and sun, unwearied rays ye dart;
Thou, humble earth, art labouring heart and soul
  To bear and cherish growth in every part;
You, juicy plants, do furnish forth the mart
  With plenty both for platter and for bowl;
Ye racing rivers vein the world-wide chart,
  While you, sweet winds, make cheer from line to
    pole.
So dances on the world.   Shalt thou, my heart,
  Be slack with sloth—idle as any fole?
Nay, rather, horsed by Heaven as thou art,
  Spring lightly to thy charioteer's control,
Or surely thou shalt feel the lash, and smart
  Through some wide æon in eternal dole.

> ' He that hath the steerage of my course
> Direct my sail.' ROM. AND JUL.

FATHER, be by me when I come to die ;
Deal thou with me as I was wont of yore
To deal with yon toy-craft, that heedfully
I sent forth faring from the firm-set shore :
When I am launching forth on Evermore,
Come to that verge of Immortality ;
Fix me fair linen, ample, aft and fore,
Secure its threadage, lest it flap and fly ;
My rudder fast at some just angle set,
To catch what breezes are careering by ;
These temper, for Thou canst, lest billow-beat
I founder in yon vast Infinity ;
But most, I pray Thee, then to hold in hand
A line, to draw me somewhere safe to land.

SHIP TO TUG.

νήνεμος αἴθρη.

Hom.

STRUGGLING with score of sails I barely strain
In painful progress o'er the windy deep;
I count me happy if across the main
Some straggling breeze shall come and kindly keep
My heavy sides from sinking into sleep;—
What is it speeds thee o'er the watery plain,
Thou mimic craft, and lends thee life to leap
And leave me, laughing at my voyage vain?
I see there is a something in thy heart
Which gives to thee a force I may not know;
To me, I pray, that secret power impart,
That I may learn some surer way to go,
Nor trust to lazy winds that puff and lull,
And leave me in the lurch, a lumbering hull.

TUG TO SHIP.

POOR ship, it grieves me sore to see thee lie
So idly murmuring on that breathless bed ;
Come, without more ado, and deftly tie
This good stout hawser 'neath thy figure-head ;
Life in my inmost heart I have, so I,
Though the wind breathe not, never feel as dead.
Come, let me draw thee with me; by-and-by
To thy fair haven thou shalt thus be sped ;
Thou art, I see, like those sad sons of men
That trust to make their way, nor look for grace ;
They start with all their goodly freight, and then,
When winds of feeling fail, they lose the race ;
But bind thyself to me, and thy desire
Shall pluck the mystery of my heart-fed fire.

> ' exitum
> Caliginosâ nocte premit deus.'
> HOR.

SWEET tenor bell,
Can any one tell,
When thy long swell
In gentle farewell
O'er knoll and o'er dell
Shall carry his knell?
    No one can tell,
    It is well, it is well.

NIGHT PRAYER BY THE SEA.

'The sea is His.'

KING of the vasty water-floods of grace,
With thee I pace beside Thy waves to-night—
My barren spirit, like this foot-marked place,
Crossed and recrossed by thoughts that were not right.
Oh, may an even, washed, and ordered space
Meet the new visit of the Day-star bright ;
To-morrow may no wandering sin leave trace
On that clear level left at morning light ;
And hear me, Heavenly Spirit, when I pray
Thy boundless love to lave me day by day;
May no unsightly flotsam lig, and bide
The sweeping refluence of Thy nightly tide;
Here, Father, let me love with Thee to walk,
And ever feel Thee smile and hear Thee talk.

Littlehampton.

THE RIME FROST.

SPIRIT who can the crystal air pervade,
I pray Thee of Thy grace forget not me :—
For in this frory network Thou hast made
Thou hast not anywhere, that I can see,
Forgotten any spray on any tree ;
Where every summer all with greeny shade
Are duly prankt of leafage dancing free,
Each sparkles stiff with thickset spangles rayed—
Am I not cased with Thy invisible air ?
Dost Thou not course my Being's branchery
With stealthy force, oh, touch my fancies bare
And me, too, clothe with such brave ministry;
My wintry life nor fig nor leaf can show—
Yet over even me Thy breath like grace might throw.

MY KEEPER OF THE KEYS.

HERE, Lord, I give Thee this poor house, my heart :
Oh, would in giving this I gave Thee more ;
Pr'ythee take full possession, whole and part,
Take large key, latch key, of my life's front door ;
Enter at will, all passages explore, ·
Undo the shuts, let air and light indart ;
Here is the key of yonder sorry store,
Lo, thine it is ; henceforth make Thou my mart :
And see this other bunch of great and small,
I yield them up—I pray Thee, take them all—
Why need I tell to Thee my curious locks,
My springs, my drawers, my warded subtleties ?
Take archives, jewel-case, and treasure-box—
Lo, all I have and am to Thee wide open lies.

DEATH THOUGHTS.

'Quum frigida mors animâ seduxerit artus.'

TERRIBLE cold, horrible heat,
I quiver and shiver from head to feet,
      Riot without rest
      Thro' brain and breast,
Something rides down the delicate cause
That has held me together sans care or pause,
Some dread destroyer of beautiful laws,
My cheek cleaves tight to my dry, hot jaws.
      The daylight goes
      For darkness to come,
      Silence upflows
      From the land of the dumb ;
As the round of my life rolls again into light
From this side I feel the upcreeping of night,
My foot will never spring from the bed
And this dull weight of my death-damp head
Lies flung back on my pillow like lead.
The night lamp flickers thro' languid lashes,
This hand will never fling up the sashes
To hear the breeze through the clump of ashes
And joy in the light with its morning flashes.

One loving face is leaning o'er me,
If love could do it, enough to recover me,
I feel her breath, but there seem, there seem,
As a vivid apathy wraps me in dream,
    Lying between her life and me
    Leagues and leagues of eternity :
    My nerve is too faint
    To hope to paint
The sorrow-swamped grace of that loving face
Upon this glazed and dwindled space ;
    A week ago
    It had made me glow
With all the joys the happiest know.

    The air of the morning
    As ever is humming,
    With musical warning
    That daylight is coming,
      But I bear no part
For the throb at my brain and the blaze at my heart.

    Soul and body play not on
    In their wonted unison,
    Spirit will no longer choose
    Spoiled and blunted tools to use ;
    Fast my body shorn of wings
    Sinks into the crypt of things,
    By the rising spirit hurled
    With the seen and handled world,

Losing now its only tie
To the seed which does not die.
Soon my spirit is of age,
And the mind that helped it on
To its timely heritage
Finds its occupation gone,
Memory, that served so well
Things that had been once to tell,
Will not any more be pleasant
To the spirit whose delight,
Self-sufficing at a sight,
Grasps the all-embracing present ;
Things that have been soon will be
Swamped in free Eternity
Reckoned with the things that are,
And the moment is not far
Things to come will so be given
As beseems the need of heaven.

The heat of the battle is over and done,
I have lost and death has won,
Though I soon shall make the boast
I have won and death hath lost,
I must now lie still and feel myself crumble,
Key stone, corner stone are gone,
The bridge has nothing left but to tumble,
But while I slip from manhood into clay
There is that is pleasant in passing away.

Helpless, painless, in my dream
I am borne away by the strength of a stream,
    Lying, dying,
No use complaining, wholly complying,
    This life closing, that unveiling,
    This life gathering, that life failing,
    Visions break on my beholding
    Things I looked for fast unfolding,
    Sweetest mysteries one by one
Stream from a background lucid in the sun,
    And now, my victory achieved,
    I see in whom I have believed.

Part the Third,

—

SUNDRY RELIQUES.

LIVE AND LET LIVE.

YE blooms by the side of the burn,
How kindly ye wait for your turn;
Some of you coming together,
Aware of your week and your weather;
But when ye have ended your story,
And shown your particular glory,
Calmly withdrawing your head,
That others may step in your stead.
Thus for a new delight of our eyes
A monthly fashion will rise;
To-day the brook-side on fire is
By the fresh rillet edges
All in the bevy of strong green sedges
With the stately, tall yellow iris,
While blue belladonna adorneth the hedges.
I marvel much how each of you wedges
Its intricate way through the rootage of those
Who have fully flowered and won their repose,
Or else are waiting to flower
Each in her season and hour;
None of you seem in the least to smother
Or hamper or carp at the growth of each other,
Ye never elbow, ye sulk not nor rush
Nor with haste unseemly push and crush;

When your bloom is over, ye sink to the breast
Of your earth to leave time and room for the rest ;
And then, when your winter bedtime has come,
Ye lie all in peace and hope in your tomb,
Tho' men call you weeds
Having shed all your seeds
By the way to be trampled by each one that passes,
Or else to enrich the next summer grasses ;
In the lap of the earth ye patiently bide
To renew the wayside next summer-tide,
Waiting your turn by the bank of the burn.

LOVE-MAKING.

I SAT and watched them—was it well?
    What right had I to tarry there?
Or, tarrying, what right to tell
    Of how she loosed her golden hair?

I watched them making youthful love;
    Close, close to him she drew her chair,
And beaming, starlike, from above,
    Caressed him with her golden hair.

With sprinkled kiss and floral scent
    She blew upon the forehead bare,
And lovingly above him bent
    And fanned him with her fragrant hair.

The rondure of her fragrant cheek
    Like wholesome fruit hung o'er him there;
She did not seem to want to speak,
    But only fanned him with her hair.

'Ah! happy youth,' you smile and say,
    'Thrice happy, in so kind an air,
To feel above you, night and day,
    The fanning of that golden hair.'

For he so young and she so fair,
  What marvel, joying in her grace,
If he should praise the golden hair
  That fanned and cooled his—*dying face?*

Ah, yes, for such the love they made,
  They made a love that knew not time ;
Whose time to flower was time to fade,
  And night came down at morning prime.

If down his brow the sorrows fell
  To warm the faint cold dews there were,
Like one of whom the Gospels tell,
  She wiped them with her golden hair.

And He whose Love makes love sublime
  By me bespoke those lovers twain,
'Love's fading time is flowering time,'
  'For love like yours will bloom again.'

TESTUDO CARA.

i.

DEAR little lady tortoise, thee I bought,
I' the early summer, baking in our street ;
Thee and thy mate, now lost, to lawn I brought
And fed thee daily with convenient meat ;
Of all such cates I thought could please thee, nought
Was left unlaid before thy house-hid feet ;
Lotus and lettuce, dandelion we sought
And watched thee reach them to thy roofed retreat ;
Full well we knew where thou wert wont to lie,
Close i' the clover or neath cope of stone ;
And, if our beldame ever and anon
Missed thee awhile, she found thee by-and-by ;
But once a sneap of winter chilled the sky,
All haunts we searched and searched—but thou wert
    gone.

ii.

Ah, me ! what lonely lot must now be thine !
Were we not fain to house thee safe and warm,
Either where kitchen fire should round thee shine,
Pet of the household, free from least alarm,
Or where the grapery's fictitious clime
Should shield thy pictured tent from pierce of harm—
Through all the comfort of our Christmas time
Why hast thou sought in solitude a charm ?
Say, was it well thy friendship to withhold
And thus forego our hospitable care ?
 Why seek a cemetery deep and cold
 So that thy dearest friends divine not where ?
Well, may kind Heaven, that gave thy manners, save
And raise thee up again from self-sought grave.

iii.

Oh, may thy fate be luckier than the lot
Of that progenitor of larger growth,
Whom Maia's son, once wandering i' the south
Found on some shore—for lyrists tell us not,
Whether by Nile, or if that curious youth
Came on him first by Lesbos ; dry and hot
The winds had withered him, and summer drouth
Had drained his life on that disastrous spot.
Across his shell some lingering chords there lay,
And, as the breezes idling off the sea
Came dreaming by, they woke a harmony
For all the lyres of the after-day,
Whereby thy forebear, suffering grievous wrong,
Made all thy kind immortal in all song.

iv.

For Mercury, so eloquent of tongue,
So light of finger, with the same deft hand
Wherewith he drove the Sun-god's herd along,
And filched the darts, whereby Apollo planned
With swift repayal to avenge his wrong—
Whereat the o'erreached Archer filled the land
With breaking smiles—I say with that same hand
Did Maia's son awake that shell to song—
Yea, by its aid he smoothed the rugged ways
Of early men ; for poets rose and sung
And filled the air with soul-subduing lays
Which since through Hellas and the world have rung.
Oh, that in time that youth's divining rod
May lead thy life from ground back to our sunny sod.

NIGHT SONG OF VECTIS.*

I FEEL like a babe in its rest
  Rocked on the lap of the sea,
Her arms hold me up to her breast
  As loving and close as can be.

At the fall of the rosy red even
  The breath that she sends to the sky
Spun into garments of heaven
  Swathes me in vermily.

And all the day, all the night long,
  Ever unwearily,
Round me with music and song
  She chanteth my lullaby cheerily.

Round me the song of my mother
  Has arisen kind from my birth ;—
The wind song is just such another
  That plays round the isle of the earth.

I lie on the lap of the sea,
  And look the far worlds in the face,
As the world that we dwell in may be
  Rocked on the bosom of space.

Freshwater.

* Isle of 'Wight.'

THE ALBAN LAKE.

CHANGELESS Thyself, how sweet the changes are
Thy fancy plays upon the chimes of things !
When here the moods of Nature are at war
Her bursting heart what reckless anguish wrings ;
Swayed by the tempests' hundred hurtling wings
Fires, like her lifeblood, gushed from yonder scar
And leaped with clamours wild from earth to star :
What rest becalmed those ancient sorrowings ?
Hot-throated hills, now pleasant woodlands screen you,
And bright and blue the lake that sleeps between you,
Now for those quenchings of the day's fair face
Your skies and waters answer grace for grace —
Ah, God ! who lovest peace and hatest war,
Thyself unchanged, how good thy changes are !

WINTER ROSES.

i.

ALTHOUGH your tresses gleam with grey,
   The roses rest upon your cheek,
And though you wear a matron's way,
   Your lips can glance, your eyes can speak,
And still there plays the ancient grace
Old men remember in your face.

ii.

The broadsides of how many years
   Have aimed to bear your charm away,
But that sweet pennon still appears
   Beyond the range of all their play,
And waves, as Love had nailed it fast,
Serene upon your gallant mast.

iii.

Time was, I hear my betters say,
   When other brows could rival thine,
But those have gathered day by day
   Some bitter writing line on line,
Whether some hurt has caught the mind,
Or else their heart was not so kind.

iv.

Yet thou, as fair as they at first,
   Hast found the calm of peace within,
And sorrow thus hath wrought her worst
   And best, without her sister, sin,
While hourly love and daily duty
With grace for grace enhance thy beauty.

v.

Those meaner souls must pass through fire
   And have their features half unwrought
To undecypher wrong desire
   And cancel traits of restless thought ;—
When thou full angel com'st to be
That angel must resemble thee.

vi.

I knew thee not in earlier days,
   Nor saw thee when thy prime was young,
Or, certes, in my warmer lays,
   Thou hadst not gone so long unsung,
But let that light upon thy brow,
Lady, accept this homage now.

THE RHENISH MAIDEN.

TELL me, O love, whose happy genius plays
The same fond phantasy a thousand ways,
Why doth yon Rhenish maiden choose to bear
The silver arrow in her golden hair?
Was such the speed wherewith her lover flew,
Where eve by eve their genial friendship grew?
Or doth it token that the shaft she drew
Drove to her mark unwaveringly true,
And, tipped with passion, clove one heart in two,
Till two thus cloven became one anew?
  Thus as a Siegfried, when his wars were done,
His vassals victors and new vassals won,
Beheld the spear that made the foemen fall,
And hung the trophy in his castle hall—
So she, at length, her bloodless battles over,
Plucks the good arrow from her kneeling lover,
Bears it aloft in that her golden braid,
And reigns, in heart a wife, in hand awhile a maid.

Frankfort.

ECLIPSE OF THE MOON

(Aug. 23, 1877).

YE pretty stars, it pricks me to the core
   To see you gathered round your mistress' head ;
Yea, verily, it moveth me right sore
   To mark your being thus discomfited.
What ! will your gracious mistress never more
   Walk forth for you ? and is she quite, quite dead ?
Hath she whose majesty ye wont to adore
   Foregone for ever that her queenly stead ?
How kind ye are ; with what solicitude,
   I note, ye trim your small sepulchral wicks ;
Nor do ye spare a kind infinitude
   Of pains your lights to circle or to fix ;
Maybe it was your Lady's last, last hest
   When she was gone to burn your little best.

CLAUDIA.

(DEDICATED TO THE PEOPLE OF BOGNOR.)

WHAT time the State of Rome began to grow,
'Twas told by the report of oracle,
That she could only flower to Empery
If in the girdle of her walls there came
The goddess of Pessinus.   Whereupon
They sent their noblest on an embassage
To crave her marble form from Phrygia
(Whereof Pessinus was a little town) :—
' Cousins,' said these, ' were they, of the whole blood,
Sprung of the lordliest of the Phrygian lords,
Æneas.'   Upon this that kindly folk
Let go their goddess.   So with heedful joy
They laid her gently in the sunny lap
Of a fair ship to bring her home to Rome.
But, when in course they came to Tiber mouth,
It seemed the pure divinity that lay
Immarbled there was heavy and displeased
By reason of some wrong, they knew not what.
Howe'er it was, the conscious ship stood still,
And that, although the West implored her sail,
And the importunate waves, running apace,
On their white shoulders would have lifted her;
They haled, they strained—the stoutest arms in Rome
Tugged, till one said the very prow of her
Would part—and yet she stirred never an inch.

It chanced, if chance it was, the selfsame day
There was a maid of Vesta's nunnery,
Claudia by name, sweet as a violet,
Whom some lewd fellows of the baser sort
In low-tongued babble, gloating on some lie—
Some garbage in the sewage of their slums—
First low, then loud, charged with a deed of shame.
Of this she rightly recked not, till she found
That, like a swollen drain, they hurried her
To that Tarpeian rock, from whose high crag
They hurled frail vestals.   Then she rose and spake,
While all the ribald folk fell back from her:
'What I have done—why you, oh, men, do this,
I know not.   Pessinuntia be my judge.'
Then all the people said: 'Let her be judged
By Pessinuntia.'   So they led her down
To where the ship stood fast at Tiber-mouth.
And here she loosed the band that girded her
'Neath the fair place of snowy hemispheres
Unsullied ever by a print of sin—
And held it streaming forth and fluttering
All in the air of heaven, and straightway said
In hearing of them all, goddess and men,
Praying aloud: 'Oh, mother of the gods,
To whom my heart is known if innocent,
If guilty, known; if I be found by thee
To be as one of thine—come on to Rome.'
And then she wound her girdle in a noose,

And catching loosely the gay prow thereby
Held it aloft with airy finger-tip,
Like one that tices more than one that draws.
Before her sash could lose its light festoon,
Lo! what befel; for that obedient craft—
Much like a swan that hastens to be fed,
When some sweet child holds bread upon the bank—
Came after her so willing, that the waves
Of that dread stream that swallowed Silvia,
With merry music round about the prow,
Danced up in curvy founts, with silvery crest,
Pleased to the ground to ope a way for her.
This was because the goddess, who was there,
Knew what she knew; and what she knew was this:
That that young Vestal was as white in soul
As she was beautiful to look upon.
Then all the people came about the maid,
Rejoicing with a tumult of delight,
And all made holiday the whole day long,
Hailing the fair oracular augury
Of Empery with Pessinuntia.

TO A PARISIAN ACTRESS

(who used after the play to carry her earnings for the starving children of her blanchisseuse, whom, without the knowledge of any one else, she nursed through an illness).

THAT deed was gracious as the shower at night,
Which none have witnessed but the thoughtful sky,
The stars, and moon, if chance they caught the sight,
And the kind angels that were oaring by,
Heaven's couriers bent on kindred ministry;
For had not they attained that happy height
Because in love they took a long delight?
And shalt not thou be one with those on high?
The still shower stole into the garden's bosom,
The buds, that hung a-dying, rose to blossom;
Nor till the morn could tell the Providence
Of that true dream of mute benevolence;
Its gentle deed of loving-kindness done,
The shower stole back to heaven to meet the morning
     sun.

'Ελελιζομένη διεροῖς μέλεσιν.

Ar.

SOME bird is warbling for my joy, but where
   I weet not : wistfully I gaze
Through all the tremulous rounds of leafage there ;
   All ear and eye about me, lo ! I raise
Peering inquiry from my fount of praise—
   That half-articulate sonneter, too rare
To be commended in elaboured lays.
   Ah, me ! I fail to find her anywhere ;
Blest could I know who blesses me.   'Tis so
   I prove the sweet effects of some kind soul,
Whose wishes waft about me as I go ;
   I feel some hidden help doth make me whole.
How like that sightless song this soundless prayer !
Some one is praying for me :—tell me, Where ?

RESURGAM.

WE lit upon her laid in Tiber ooze,
  Discountenanced with centuries of slime ;
All form and feature seemed, alas ! to lose
  What trace she once had known of touch sublime ;
What thrifty man but straightway might refuse,
  Counting it reckless waste of golden time,
So cheap and cumbersome a thing to choose
  For aught but binding highways with her lime ?
But we were idle ; so we laved her face,
  And whitened limb by limb with growing care,
When, lo ! a resurrection of rare grace !
  What majesty divine ! what queenly air !
And now she stands aloft in honoured place,
  And men repeat her beauty everywhere.

THE TWO WAVES OF THE YEAR.

My pippins, shall your bloom and blossom die?
Mark we no more your pink-white promise blow
Against the dark-blue hills and bright blue sky?
What mean ye? must we lose all heart or no?
This green shows flat and cold to our spoiled eye,
Missing your upflung shower of vermeil snow;
And much our pleasure it imports to know
If aught will else betide you by-and-by?
Ah! grace be with your growing! now I see
Your bloom was but the crest of a first wave;
When breaks the next, a fairer sight will be,
The fruit of this that falls to grassy grave,
For rich red glorious globes will soon fulfil
Your hidden promise against sky and hill.

κάλυκος λοχεύματα.

Æsch.

I FEEL within my mind, as feels the world,
Certain and not uncertain of its way,
Much as a flower, methinks, might feel encurled
In the green swathing-bands of mystery ;
Surely a strange sweet pleasure there must be
To find its veiling fold by fold unfurled ;
What curious hope to open out and be
One with the bloomings of the higher world.
To grow in God has something sweet for me
Beyond all utterance of my mother speech ;
Certain of what I know, I cannot see
Beyond a widening range within my reach ;
The known gives courage for my hope to flow,
While what I know not brightens what I know.

THE MEDITERRANEAN BY NIGHT.

(A FRAGMENT.)

UP, up, up, where the spires of the cypresses quiver—
Down, down, down, where the olive-yards drink of the
river—

Back and away far back where the last little home-
stead light
Gleams like a glowworm on terraces guarding the
wine-dark height.

The vine-dresser taketh his rest, and knoweth not
whence nor how
Heavier swing his bunches of purpling wealth on the
bough.

Praise to the Lord who can charm the rains into colour
and shape,
And enchant from the dust of the earth the delicate
blood of the grape.

Yon vein of golden milk that the breast of heaven
pervades
Falls to the sea and the olives, spilling itself in the
shades ;

On, on, on, till you verily dare not denay
The opening fires of night to be sinking fires of day,

Peer with what eyes you may, you tell not whether
       they be
Stars in the limitless sky or lights on the limitless sea ;

For the clustering communes are shining on high like
       hamlets of stars,
And the arabesques overhead run down to the sea-
       watched Phares.

AN OLD MAN TO HIS OLD DOG.

i.

ASSOCIATE of my latest years,
   Kind comrade of my path of fate,
With me you trudge—it so appears—
   Close up to my immortal gate ;
Abroad I roam—I sit at home—
I go, you go ; I come, you come.

ii.

Down there before our common hearth
   As rug on rug you loosely lie,
A negligence of curly worth—
   Say must you leave me when we die ?
Upon mine hours, mine eyes you wait,
And we are moving to the gate.

iii.

I do not care, I own, to face
   The thought that if I first depart
The power that does me that last grace
   Will ever find it in his heart
To ope the wicket wide for me
And straightway shut it back on thee.

iv.

To-night I closed our dwelling-door,
   But left thee in the dark and cold ;
The bolt was barely home before
   That sad mischance you fearless told ;
Thy sharp and quick indignant din
Imperious clamoured, 'Let me in.'

v.

And so, methinks, 'twill be that day,
   When we th' eternal portals reach ;
For should the Porter say you nay
   You will so beg and so beseech ;
Lavish your tricksiest tricks you'll give
And 'die' to be allowed to live.

THE MASSACRE OF THE INNOCENTS.

HEAPED on their bier for bearing to their tomb—
Ah, woeful massacre of innocent lives—
A withering barrow-load of daisy-bloom
To morn beheaded by revolving knives;
To me each flower is dear where'er it thrives,
For them as well as me the earth had room;
What means this wont of gardeners, that drives
My lawn's best beauty to this wasteful doom?
This iron order of invisible law
Revolves how full of unexpressive sorrow,
These eyes of day, when Day's Eye last they saw,
Little they recked of what should chance the morrow,
No more than those young tumbled heads of them
In baskets by thy gates, Jerusalem.

BOATS AND BIRDS.

WHAT are these that past me scurry?
Little ships in homeward hurry,
Hieing with the wind and tide
Deep i' the haven for to hide ;
Lo ! they shoot themselves at last
In among where many a mast
Rising mid the streamside trees
In expectant argosies
Wait the shipman's purposes ;
From their moon-loved deeps they come,
Glad to find their evening home,
Many a little darkling sail,
Bosomed by the landward gale,
Bears them right on yon soft bank,
Where, when they have ta'en their rank,
Down they drop their tan-black wings
To rest, like other evening things.
   So at nightfall taking stand
Nigh some water locked by land
You may watch the grebe and coot
With the dusky waterhen,
For their bedtime is afoot,
When they've done their daylong story
Haste in quest of nest again

Thwart the moon's broad path of glory ;
So they vie in sedgeward race
While their wing-tips flip the face
Of the black resplendent glass,
So to the covert safe of their tall reeds they pass,
So shake and furl their small dark sails,
And hide their sleepy bills beside their cosy tails.

Witham bank, Boston.

LUGGER TO EAGER.*

Hail to thee, herald of the ocean's flow,
I love to hear thy gallant galloping on,
My drooping pennon now takes heart, for, lo !
I see what I have hoped ; I mark thee don
That curling crest ; the hours went sadly slow
Till I could hear thy dancing antiphon ;
I cannot bide to feel the freshets go,
For with each downset ebb my time is gone.
Here have I laid me sidelong on the ooze,
Falling as fell the rain-replenished tide,
How could I rest me in my natural pose,
Or dance as wont or watch my mirrored pride ?
I bent in helpless case my sorry head
Without thy waters round me, idle as the dead.

Boston.

* The 'bore' in the river Witham.

'THE WINTER OF OUR DISCONTENT.'

'Damna tamen celeres reparant cœlestia lunæ.'

HOR.

WE think too little when the year seems dead
Of those potential charms that wait below;
The earth fares wet and naked; overhead
The grey and ill-conditioned tempests blow;
Life looks a failure in the land, and so
We sigh and think that nothing good has sped;
What meets the eye is all akin to woe,
Quite ragged, rugged, and discoloured—
Lord, what poor babes we be—not for to know
That there is nought so hopeful as the dead,
That for sweet nature in this guise to go
Is the best token of her Princelihead,
That in that cratch of Bethlehem to be
Was the dear Lord's divinest irony.

'Αριθμὸν ἔξοχον σοφισμάτων.

Æsch.

'I am ill at these numbers.'

HAMLET.

O NUMBER, thou finger with skeleton bone,
At thy touch all the spirit of Beauty is flown—
Shall I cut dry and letter the aspects of Truth?
Shall I label and docket the flowers of Youth?
Shall I decimal blessings that drop from above?
Shall I count all the kisses I shower on my Love?
Shall I vivisect life till I find it to be
A dead-a-live question of one, two, and three?
My hopes for Eternity, say—shall I fix,
If the reasons for Heaven are found to be six?
Except for to reckon my beggarly pence,
Number, I need thee not; hence, pr'ythee hence.

ἒν πρὸς ἒν
ἔργον δυνάμει μετρεῖται.

Arist.

WHEN to yon fopless world your course has come,
Much I misdoubt if quite you'll feel at home,
For, lady, there what flaws will you detect
Which here your prime delight is to correct?
Nor will your guise in that abode of bliss
Find scope to look so charming as in this ;
For know you ne'er evince such heavenly grace
As when you slap some coxcomb in the face,
Nor ever seem you so supremely sweet
As when some fool lies bleeding at your feet.

   Howe'er it be, 'twill all be ordered well ;
Is there not heaven and heaven, hell and hell?
Thus there will be provided, it may hap,
Some constant face for hands like yours to slap,
Your very grace and glory it may be
To scourge and purge souls lost in foppery.

TO A FORGOTTEN IDEA.

i.

AH, phantom fancy, dead before thy birth,
Into what fields of faery art thou flown?
Why didst thou never foot the solid earth
Nor let me grasp and name thee for mine own?
Brief embryo, yet mine, sans flesh, sans bone,
Faint nebula, sans pole and heart and girth,
Though I could never clip thee with a zone—
How can I wholly treat thy death with mirth?
Had I but held this little pencil then,
So had I saved thee from to lapse again
To hybernate with larvæ, shapeless, cold,
Into the crypt of things that are not told;
Come, airy thought, return, return, I pray;
Surely I ne'er again will say thee nay.

ii.

I trace indeed some record dim of thee,
Two avenues there were, that there and then
Promised, I mind me, some true harmony ;
Thou wast a thought that had not come to men,
And may not ever visit them again;
In form thou wast some clear analogy
That lit a doubtful region to my ken,
The resolute shaming of some fallacy :—
To draw forth tablets seemed a needless task,
Thou wast so pure and simple when I met thee,
I thought e'en my frail wit could ne'er forget thee,
My memory methought I need but ask ;
But now I plunder all my mind in vain
To lure thee, Sibyl, with that leaf again.

iii.

Come, dear my thought, and coming wider ope
The wicket of that large and fecond space
Where yet unlinked with mind, and hour, and place,
Thou and thy sisters have eternal scope ;
What are ye ? Star-like nuclei of hope,
Beams from the eyes that light the eternal face,
Ye bide to be entrapped in type and trope
To turn your wealth on this slow-headed race ;
Lingering, I pray thee, with thy kind right hand
Fix wide with one firm push the said small gate
That gives from yonder spiritual land,
So will I plant myself thereby and wait ;
Who knows but many a thought to meet my need
Will follow on, taking thy gracious lead ?

PEACE.

From the *Spectator*.

πολεμοῦμεν ἵν᾽ εἰρήνην ἄγωμεν.

Arist.

PEACE will carry many a sign
That is not her proper choice ;
Peace will utter many a line
That is not her proper voice ;
Standing in her battle-car
Leaning o'er the storms of war.

Is it peace, will some one say,
This that wears the air of war ?
Yes—her feelings, thoughts, to-day
Are but as they ever are ;
She in whom your souls delight
See her in her robe of might.

See how all her wonted ways
Perish in her fiery mood,
Hollow votaries shrink to gaze
On her beauty dashed with blood ;
All the true around her press
Love her rather more than less.

Go, regard her clouded front,
Mark her with her clenched palm,
Spurning, other than her wont,
All the happy works of calm ;
With that warcloud on thy brow,
Peace, I'll love thee then as now.

Peace alone is rightly strong,
Peace alone is truly just ;
'Tis because she hates the wrong
That she loves the battle dust ;
When the fret of wrong is past,
Peace at first is peace at last.

Lamb-like, when her laws allow,
When the nations guard the right,
Peace is like a lion now
Ravening for the splendid fight ;
So goes forth when battle burns,
Lamb-like still when she returns.

Peace abhorreth them that sit
Smiling by the factory porch,
Though they see the welkin lit,
Though they smell the battle torch,
Heeding not how ruin fares
So there blaze no bales of theirs.

When the sordid purple clique
Tread their folk to dust at will,
Hast thou ne'er a word to speak ?
Ne'er a duty to fulfil ?
Till the sceptred robbers cease
What hast thou to do with Peace ?

Let the tyrant plainly see,
Let him tremble as he knows
That is not the whole of thee
That magnificent repose !
That when wisdom gives the word,
Britain, all thy strength is stirred.

Ye who truly love and serve
This fair image of delight,
Throw your soul in every nerve,
Up and rally for the fight,
Turn your yardwands into swords,
For the battle is the Lord's.

How shalt Thou be rightly named ?
We are sore divided, Father,
Till the wrong be throughly shamed,
Whether we must call Thee rather
In the low earth's rebel coasts
Prince of Peace or God of Hosts.

Father, whose transcendent voice
Speaketh all the peace it may,
E'er our god-like power of choice
Fiend-like fling Thy peace away,
Flow into the nation's heart,
Be the God of Peace Thou art.

Part the Fourth.

HYMNS.

WEDDING HYMN.

WELLHEAD of Being, central Heart,
  Eternal Fount of Light and Grace,
Oh, may we see Thee as Thou art
  In fulness of our Saviour's face!
Spirit in whom we live and move,
Unseal, refresh our springs of Love.

May seeds of Life eternal sown
  So prove their good and honest ground,
That in our hearts to ripeness grown
  Good fruit an hundredfold be found;
May these Thou makest man and wife
Be heirs of all the grace of life.

Grant that, as hand is joined with hand,
  So heart may grow with heart enwound,
And both be conscious of a band
  Of golden love about them bound,
Whereof this ring is pledge and sign
By vow and promise, theirs and Thine.

May these whom Thou and Love unite
  In bond more happy than the free
Neither below nor in the height
  By chance or change asundered be;
Full term of union may they see
Each with the other, both with Thee.

To plight the troth and give the hand,
  As here before our face they kneel,
That Day may both together stand,
  Their forehead radiant with Thy seal,
Among the blest, by Jesu known,
Before Thee on the great White Throne.

April, 1886.

HARVEST HYMN.

LORD, in grateful adoration,
   Lo, we bend before Thy face;
Landlord of the great Creation,
   Grant, we pray Thee, grace for grace.

Rain and sun Thou duly gavest,
   Seed to sow and heart to till;
Now again our life thou savest—
   Miracles of mercy still.

Twice the thousands hungered round Thee,
   Hearing what Thy love would say;
Little had they, but they found Thee
   Loth to send them faint away.

So Thou bidd'st the willing season
   Take the scanty seed we throw,
And, unread by mortal reason,
   Feed our hungry thousands now.

Harvest passing, summer ending,
   Sin o'ercome and sorrow braved,
Grant, we pray before Thee bending,
   We and ours at last be saved.

HYMN FOR ALL SAINTS' DAY.

PRAISE Him, world without beginning,
   First that left our Father's hand,
Primal souls unsoiled by sinning
   Ere the younger Earth was manned;
Ye the full-come kingdom share,
Praise Him, all ye saints that were.

Praise Him, world that now is going
   Wrapt in dusty raiment still;
Purer than we dream of, glowing
   Like the snows on early hill:
True the vision, though afar—
Praise Him, all ye saints that are.

Praise Him, world with judgment ending,
   Praise him, ye that shall be born;
Clouds of souls henceforth ascending
   Ever till the general morn;
Wider, wiser Church I see—
Praise Him, all ye saints to be.

Way, and truth, and life discerning
   Are they few whom Christ has saved?
Christ an answer now returning
   Points to those His love has laved;
Oh that, as Time's river rolls,
All the saints were all the souls!

CONCEALMENT.

IF all were open and plain, oh, mother, what would I
 give !
I'm sure if I made it die, 'twas in trying to make it
 live ;
Robert—indeed, indeed—your love it has hurt me sore,
'Twere well had you loved me less ; 'twere best had
 you loved me more ;
'Twere better a thousand times you had hated me
 worse than hell,
For then I had shunned your way, but you seemed
 to love me so well.
I know not how it befell ; he bewitched and mastered
 me then ;
How small was the price I got to be never happy again ;
Something within kept saying, ' Oh, why did you come
 with him here ?'
But faint I was with love and confused all over with
 fear.
My mistress kindly said, ' Oh, Hannah, poor girl, I fear
You've got into trouble sore,' and she pressed my hand
 with a tear.

Although at the moment I spoke I felt a throb at my
    side,
I looked in my mistress' face and opened my lips and
    lied :
If only they knew my mind, Oh, Heaven, what would
    I give ;
Oh, how could they ever think I could wish that it
    should not live?
Wringing my hands together, I tried to smother my
    moan ;
Oh, mother, had you been there ! it was hard to bear it
    alone ;
Indeed it was hard to bear ; it was worse than being
    alone,
For He was with me then who knew the things I had
    done.
If all were but known to all, oh, mother, what would
    I give?
I'm sure, if I made it die, 'twas in trying to make it live ;
I looked in its innocent face, it uttered a feeble cry,
I pressed it once to my heart, and then I beheld it die.
And yet I might have seen it was better for it and for me
That, being born as it was, my baby should cease to be ;
But still its living smile would have made it open and
    clear
That I have not done the deed for which they have
    flung me here ;
It was almost time to milk ; I felt my way by the wall,
And I dreaded at every step I should raise the house
    by my fall ;

Oh, sweet little baby girl that was never to come to
church,

I dropped it deep in the hole at the roots of the silver
birch ;

I caught as I once looked back the bark in the water
shine,

I fainted and fell, for it seemed like the ghost of that
babe of mine.

My breast runs over with life—my heart runs over with
love,

My babe that should draw them both is now below and
above.

I flung my heart to the skies in a horrible anguish of
prayer,

I looked for a God of love, but an angry God was there.

It's not for the dark or the shame ; but, oh God, it
drives me wild

To think they should think I could kill my own little
innocent child.

Robert, oh, Robert, your love indeed it has grieved me
sore ;

Oh, would you had loved me less ; oh, would you had
loved me more !

www.ingramcontent.com/pod-product-compliance
Lightning Source LLC
Chambersburg PA
CBHW030600270326
41927CB00007B/994